HOW TO MAKE YOUR LIFE WORK

OR

WHY AREN'T YOU HAPPY?

BY

KEN KEYES, JR.

AND

BRUCE (TOLLY) BURKAN

ILLUSTRATED BY L. E. ANDERSON

Living Love Center
Berkeley, California

First Printing: March, 1974   15,000 copies
Second Printing: November, 1974   25,000 copies
Third Printing: November, 1975   10,000 copies
Fourth Printing: October, 1976   15,000 copies

LIVING LOVE CENTER
1730 La Loma Avenue
Berkeley, California 94709

Dedicated with love to
HILDA CHARLTON
who has given her life love and light to everyone

When you are given a gift,
it often comes with directions.
A stereo comes with an instruction book;
a car with an operator's manual.

Your life is a gift.

Would you like to know how to make your life work?

WE MEAN REALLY WORK WELL?

*No more anxiety, anger, fear, jealousy,
irritation, resentment, boredom, suffering,
unhappiness . . .*

You don't think it's possible, do you?

HA!

*It's just because you were never given the
directions with which to do it.*

*Your first step in learning how to do it is to
realize that the way you now try to improve
your life will ALWAYS keep you bouncing like
a yo-yo between happiness and unhappiness.*

*If you are not CONTINUOUSLY HAPPY—100%
of the time—it means that you are simply
stumbling through life and not taking full
advantage of the potential which has been
locked in your head since the time you were
born.*

Do you know even one person who is CONTINUOUSLY HAPPY?

If you do, that person is using his "higher consciousness." People who continually use their "higher consciousness" **NEVER** *experience the disappointment of unfulfilled expectations.*

We know you try hard.
We know you're a good person.

So what's wrong?

*People who are unhappy don't know why they
are unhappy—*
if they knew why unhappiness happens,
*they would start correcting the situation so
that they would be happy—*
BUT THEY DON'T . . .
BECAUSE THEY DON'T KNOW WHAT
CAUSES *UNHAPPINESS.*

The **cause** *of unhappiness is not a mystery . . .*

It's actually quite simple.

Since you have read this far,
*perhaps you are now ready to study the **cause***
of unhappiness—ALL unhappiness—
so you can get on with being happy 100% of
the time . . .
YES, 100% OF THE TIME . . .
even in situations that used to make you
miserable [sickness, money shortage,
calamity, uncaring people, lost love, etc. etc. etc.]

Ready?

It will sound so simple that you may dismiss it all too quickly——

without really understanding how it applies to the very special conditions of your particular life.

*BUT DOING IT IS NOT SO SIMPLE—
IT TAKES A STRONG MAN OR A STRONG
WOMAN.*

Here it is.

You **automatically** *trigger feelings of unhappiness when the people and situations around you DO NOT FIT YOUR EXPECTATIONS. In other words, EXPECTATIONS create your unhappiness. It's your emotion-backed demands that make you suffer—it's not the world, the people around you or even you YOURSELF!*

Let's call these demands and expectations **"ADDICTIONS."**

An **ADDICTION** is something conditioned into
your body or mind which,
if not satisfied, **automatically** triggers a
negative emotion . . .
anger, fear, jealousy, anxiety, resentment,
sorrow, etc. etc. etc.

ALL EMOTION-BACKED DEMANDS ARE ADDICTIONS,
AND ADDICTIONS ARE THE **SOLE** CAUSE OF
UNHAPPINESS!!!

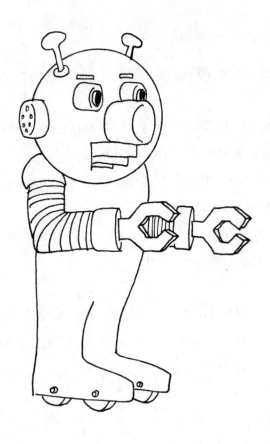

Who told you that you must automatically act like a robot and get uptight if the outside world does not fit your inner programming?

Are you going to let the world and the people around you control your life?

Do you let your happiness depend totally on the outside world?

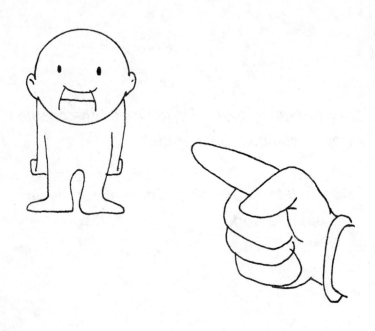

*The outside world can never **make** you unhappy—*

Only YOU can create your unhappiness.

For example . . .

YOU really don't have to UPSET YOURSELF if someone criticizes you.

There's no law which requires YOU to be afraid of anything and TRIGGER the emotion of fear, inadequacy or anger.

YOU don't have to MAKE YOURSELF irritated if the people you are with don't do what they promised.

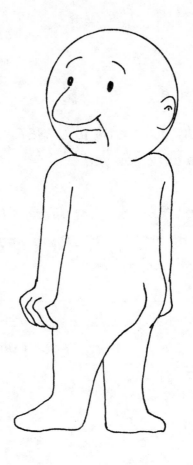

You've probably been spending your life trying to manipulate the outside world in order to be happy.

Well, has it worked?

Are you happy 100% OF THE TIME?

Have you ever succeeded in CONTROLLING THE WORLD to such a degree that it could not make you unhappy and could never again make you unhappy at any time in the future?

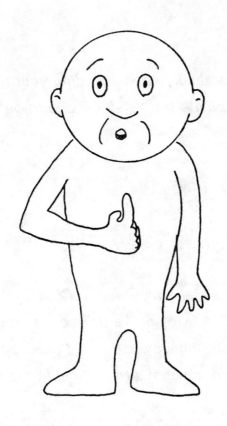

Your ego tells you that people are DOING IT to you.

But you are really DOING IT to yourself!

When you get into the science of happiness, you learn that there is [1] the outside event, and there is [2] your inside programming, which determines your RESPONSE TO THE OUTSIDE EVENT.

You know how life is—you win some and you lose some. And when you lose sufficiently often, you can generate lots of suffering in your life.

This is because you have not trained your biocomputer [your mind] so that it will NOT automatically trigger anger, fear or unhappiness when the people and things around you do not fit the elaborate programming you have stored in your head . . .

Perhaps no one ever fully explained how you can use that marvelous biocomputer to do the job properly . . . after all, every computer requires some operating skill to make the best use of all the wonderful things which it can do.

The society in which you were raised led you to believe that you could "win" consistently enough to live a happy life if you had:
   more money . . .
   or more prestige . . .
   or more knowledge . . .
   or more hobbies . . .
   or more sex partners . . .
   or more "stuff" that you can buy in stores .

YOU REALLY ACCUMULATED A LOT OF "STUFF", DIDN'T YOU?

So, are you always happy? **ALWAYS?** Are you really in love with living? Are you in love with the prospect of facing each and every new day of your life?

Each new day can be an interesting adventure. So let's learn how to enjoy every new day . . . ALWAYS! ALL WAYS!

You kept yourself in a tizzy trying to make it in life by getting people and situations to fit your inner programs of security, sensation and power [pride, prestige, ability to manipulate and control].

My how you've tried!

The way in which you try to solve one problem in your life usually creates the next problem in your life.

Lonely? Your rational mind might suggest that you need more money so that you can attract friends and lovers into your life.

You switch to a better paying job!

Now you have added business worries . . .

So your business worries keep you from relaxing and enjoying friends and lovers . . .

Do you have an ulcer yet?

When you work hard to acquire "something" to
*make you happy—**and you get it**—*
do you then worry about
losing it or damaging it?
Will it ever become obsolete?
Wouldn't you like another one?
. . . a bigger one? . . . a better one?

Do you really want to know how to get the world outside of your head to harmonize with the world inside?

It's so simple.

INSTEAD OF WEARING YOURSELF OUT
TRYING TO CHANGE THE PEOPLE AND
SITUATIONS IN YOUR LIFE, JUST
CONCENTRATE ON CHANGING YOUR
ADDICTIONS . . . YOUR DEMANDS AND
EXPECTATIONS—YOUR "ABSOLUTE
NECESSITIES" . . .

THIS IS THE **ONLY WAY** TO CONSISTENTLY
GET THE OUTSIDE AND THE INSIDE TO
HARMONIZE TOGETHER.

It is impossible to have enough money or power to change the outside world to consistently fit your inner addictions and demands. Billionaires and emperors never succeeded in finding happiness by changing the world.

Look at Napoleon.

Look at Hitler.

They couldn't do it. They tried like no one else in history, but they still couldn't do it.

The outside world can never give you "enough" if you are programmed to always want something you don't already have or more of what you do have.

If you always want "more" you will NEVER have "enough."

If you are free from addictions you can still have mild preferences. You can prefer that something happen a certain way, but if it doesn't happen, you still remain happy—because it is not a condition for your happiness.

*If it **does** happen . . . FINE!*

The game is to set things up in your head so that either way, YOU CAN'T LOSE!

It never occurs to most people that this simple solution is the only way to do it!

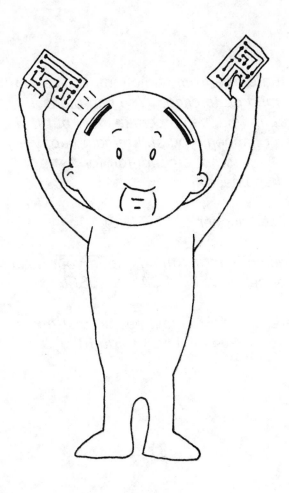

Let's view all this with a little perspective.

Isn't it easier to change your programming than to change people and situations to continuously fit your programming . . . those patterns which create demands and expectations . . . **ADDICTIONS***!?!*

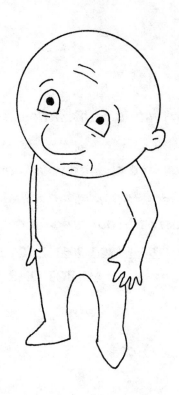

"But can't I ever try to change the outside world?"

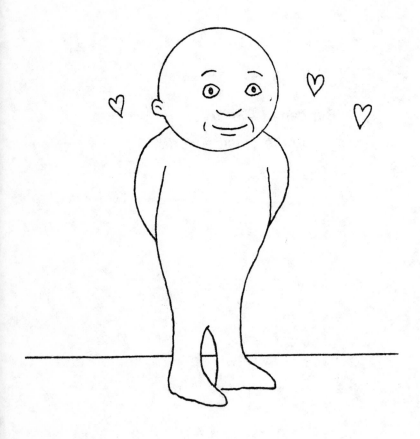

SURE!

Just use **loving communication** . . .
but don't be **addicted** *to someone or*
something changing.
If they can flow with your gentle, loving
communication, then you can
change people and situations in
a way that does not have any backlash to
create unhappiness in your life.

But your loving communication must be made with vibrations which indicate that you accept and love them unconditionally—regardless of whether they do what you prefer or not. They must feel completely free and not experience any kind of pressure from you . . . either subtle or gross.

And if your loving communication does not produce change—you still remain happy because you are not addicted to the results of your actions. You view life as a game and are not obsessed with winning or losing—you simply enjoy playing.

If you're not addicted to "winning," there is no way you can ever create the experience of loss.

Higher consciousness means enormous flexibility.
You become a master at accepting what was
previously unacceptable.

Emotional acceptance does not necessarily
mean that you have to go on someone else's
trip in the game of life.
It just means that you don't get uptight with
their trip, no matter what their trip is.
You realize that it is okay for them to do their thing—
even though you may not want to be involved
in doing it yourself.

So now you know how to make your life work.
Instead of continually striving and fighting to
change and manipulate the outside world to fit
your inner programming,
you just learn certain "higher consciousness"
techniques that make you a master at
changing your inside programming so that it
always harmonizes with the here and now
situation in the outside world . . .

IT DOESN'T HAVE TO COINCIDE, BUT IT
MUST **HARMONIZE.**

There are no "shoulds" or "shouldn'ts" as far
as the outside world is concerned.
It is the way it is! Don't waste your energy
regretting what is here and now . . .
thinking that it **should** *be different.*
Only your programming creates "shoulds" and
shouldn'ts" . . .
In reality, they do not exist.

*If you wish to involve yourself in trying to
modify a situation,
purely from a non-addictive space,
remember that you are doing it simply because
that is your role in the GAME of life.*

Instead of spending the rest of your life
fruitlessly trying to keep the world in line with
your expectations and demands,
simply modify your programming, and
then . . . like magic,

THE WORLD FEELS GREAT!

Can it really be that simple?

Well, when you try it . . .
you will see for yourself.

The past is non-existent and the future is imaginary.

You can only live NOW . . . by being in the eternal NOW MOMENT.

If you're not making it in life right now, you probably won't be making it ten minutes from now or one day from now or . . .

People who postpone happiness are like children who try chasing rainbows in an effort to find the pot of gold at the rainbow's end. It's always receding and the faster they run, the more it eludes them.

Today is perfect. It is a day which cannot be improved upon . . . unless you are comparing it with the dead past or the imagined future— neither of which really exist now.

As long as you are continually unhappy with what is, solely because it is not like what isn't, you are going to make yourself miserable forever.

You have got to enjoy "BEING" and STOP WORRYING about "BECOMING" . . . otherwise, there is absolutely no end . . .

*Your life will **never** be fulfilled until you are happy here and now.*

"Tomorrow" always becomes "today." If you are forever looking ahead into "tomorrows," when they become "todays," you will still not enjoy them because you will be pre-occupied with dreams about "new" tomorrows. Don't spend your life missing today . . . waiting for the day you CAN be happy.

*If you are not happy **today,** what dramatic difference will come with tomorrow— especially if the routine of your present life is precisely what produced the "today" you are not happy with?*

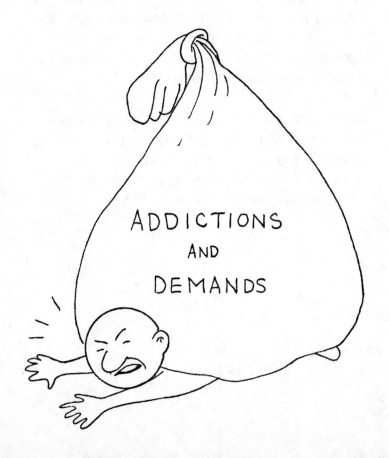

If your big, crushing bag of addictions and demands doesn't get smaller—your life can never work properly.

When will you realize that "today" **IS** *the "tomorrow" you hoped for "yesterday"?*

So why waste it looking for new tomorrows— enjoy it now because it's already yours.

The cycle of unhappiness will continue unless YOU stop it . . .

        TODAY!

Whenever your mind is preoccupied with the
rut of "pasting" or "futuring"—and your
addictions are making you reject the here and
now situation in your life—and you get uptight
and start to worry, you are depriving yourself of:

1. ENERGY. You waste energy when you
   worry about the past or future. Wanting and
   rejecting wears you out all the time.
2. INSIGHT. When you are preoccupied
   with the past or future and feel anxious or
   depressed, you may be sure that your
   insight is at its lowest point. The actions
   [or non-actions] that can create the
   optimal response to your problem will
   only occur to you when you are
   cooled-out and can see the entire
   situation with perspective. When you are
   upset, all you see with any central
   awareness is what you fear or what you
   desire.
3. LOVE. When you are caught in the grip
   of anger, jealousy, apprehension or
   resentment, you are probably throwing
   someone out of your heart or making
   yourself feel alienated from people around
   you. You are most likely turning-off the
   very people that may be most helpful to you.

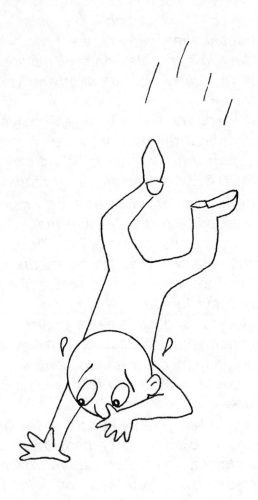

An individual who uses his higher consciousness clearly sees how addictions create the experience of suffering and alienation. The rest of us continue to wallow in self-generated and self-maintained misery. We think the people around us are causing us to be unhappy and we decide that the world around us is pretty rotten.

When we respond to the people and situations in our lives in a critical, negative, non-loving way, we tend to attract and create even more of what we don't want. This makes us even more uptight and now we are really sure that the world is at fault. We then continue spiraling downward to create tons of suffering and unhappiness in our lives.

You begin to generate happiness in your life when you free yourself from all your addictive traps.

So now you have to make a decision—

*Do you want to live the rest of your life with a brain that is full of the malignant cancers called addictions . . . emotion-backed demands, expectations, ideas of how the world **should** be, models of how people **should** treat you, etc. etc. etc.?*

Remember—YOU put this addictive programming into your head. Most of your security, sensation and power addictions were programmed by you during the first few years of your life when your biocomputer was immature and you were completely at the mercy of outside influences. What you experienced and programmed then still controls your reactions to the world today.

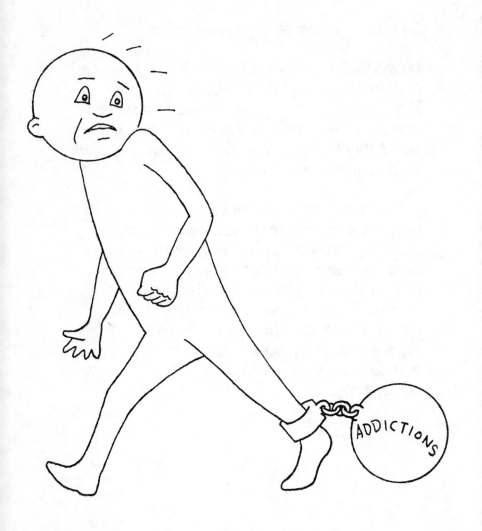

You are not your programming—
just as a computer is not its
programming . . .
When you change the programming,
the computer remains the same,
but it **operates** *differently.*

Dump your addictions!

All addictive programming
prevents you from living the happiest, most
effective life possible.

You were born with almost no programming . . .
just a few simple survival programs.
Food, air and protection from the weather
are needed to survive.

If you are not involved in meeting needs concerned with
immediate survival and you find that you are
uptight about something, you are suffering
from the "disease of demanding."

Why should you be **addicted** to something
which is not needed for survival?

ALL OTHER EMOTION-BACKED DEMANDS ARE SICKNESS!

Pretty sick world, isn't it?

Some of us are learning to free ourselves from this jail that is created by our programming and perpetuated by the involvement of our egos and rational minds.

Are YOU ready for the jail-break?

Are you strong enough for the dash to freedom? Until you realize that you have nothing to lose but your unhappiness, you won't be able to break free from the tyranny of your addictive programming . . . you'll just keep churning with feelings that make you reject what is here and now in your life.

You must realize that you can never make it in life by trying to control others.

It's a thousand times more practical to be in control of yourself.

CONTROLLING YOURSELF REALLY WORKS . . . IF YOU HAVE THE GUTS TO DO IT.

Controlling yourself does not mean that you repress your feelings. That is ulcerville.

To live effectively, peacefully and happily you must reprogram your biocomputer so that Stimulus A in the outside world does not automatically trigger Response B in you— a negative reaction to the life energies around you.

When you successfully reprogram your head, there are no more negative reactions which you have to worry about repressing.

You can now remain tuned-in, centered and loving.

Ready to do it?

Okay, let's go.

The game is to let go of all your addictions . . . uplevel your addictions [emotion-backed demands] to "preferences."

You will recall that an **addiction** *is any demand or expectation that you place upon the people and situations in your life which is backed-up by* **automatically** *triggered anger, frustration, fear, boredom, anxiety or other negative emotions.*

A **preference** *is something which you would like to have a certain way, but you will not be in the least uncomfortable if it doesn't happen that way.*

When your life is a parade of preferences, you can enjoy life all the time. When the people and situations around you do not fit your programmed preferences, it's still okay. You simply make an accepting, loving communication which says, "I love you unconditionally. It doesn't matter whether or not you fit my preferences."

When the people and situations around you happen to fit your preferences, they enable you to trigger feelings of joy, increased love, reverence, appreciation and happiness.

There's no way to lose when you uplevel addictions to preferences!

When your biocomputer is totally free from addictive programming, and only preferences remain, YOU CREATE the experience of living in a beautiful world.

When you are effectively reprogrammed, nothing can ever go "wrong." You aren't addicted to any model of how things should be in order to be "right" or "reasonable." Things are the way they are and you remain happy.

THIS IS HOW TO MAKE YOUR LIFE WORK!

It's fine to "prefer" money, education, sex, comfort or anything—but don't kid yourself into thinking it's only a "preference" if it really is an addiction. It is quite easy to tell them apart . . . will you be uncomfortable if you actually do not get the money, education, sex, comfort, etc. that you said you "preferred"?

Hm-m-m-m-m-m-m.   Remember, only **addictions** cause unhappiness.

It doesn't appear that you are yet convinced.

What are you saying?

*Are you saying that if you don't get mad,
anxious or jealous when people treat you a
certain way, they'll just run over you as if you
were a cream puff? Or if you eliminate fear
from your biocomputer are you afraid you may get hurt
in certain situations?*

*Are you wondering whether negative emotions
have a real place in life to help you avoid pain
and gradually mold people and situations so
that you can live with them comfortably?*

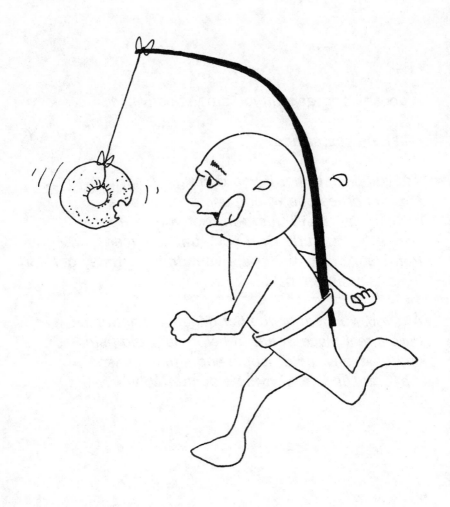

You've got an interesting point there.

If you don't respond at all to the world, the world will probably just roll over you, because it won't see you. People won't know what you prefer . . . because they aren't mind-readers.

But the problem with using negative emotions to manipulate and control the world is that they only work to a certain point. They will never enable you to control and dominate the outside world ENOUGH to give you the experience of feeling secure, to give you enough enjoyable sensations, and to give you enough effectiveness and power in your life.

Sure, if you competently manipulate, you will have more security, sensations and power than if you made no attempt at all to interact with the outside world. But they'll keep you trotting along like a donkey chasing a carrot which is dangling from a stick tied around his neck. Every now and then you may get a nibble of the carrot if it swings your way, **but you'll never get the whole carrot.** *You may have moments of pleasure, but remember, if life is working properly, you are* **continuously** *happy . . . 100% of the time.*

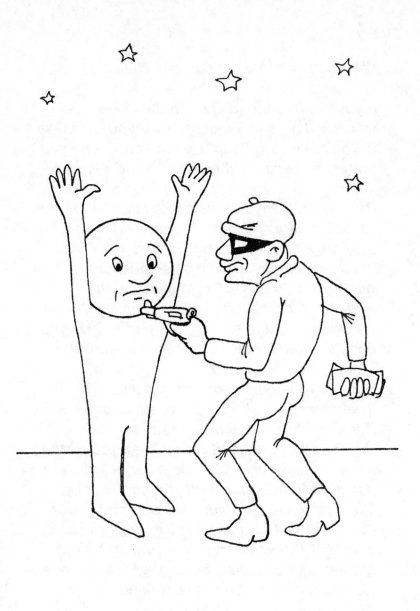

"What if I'm being attacked or am in physical danger?"

*Well, chances are pretty good that if you panic or get excited or become emotionally upset— you will not be able to think clearly and you might even act in a way which will actually contribute to your injury. If you stay centered and loving in **all** situations, you will be assured of acting from a clear headspace and will automatically react in a way that will produce the **best possible** results.* **Have you ever IMPROVED your performance by worrying** *or by making yourself unhappy because of a "here and now" situation?*

*A businessman actually does better in business when he uses the Living Love Way, simply because he is not impeded by the handicap of worry and unhappiness which both distorts his business perception and also prevents him from enjoying **every** aspect of his business and personal life.*

Remember, you are not trying to change what
you are doing . . .
only the headspace from which you do it.
The game is to do **everything** *from a tuned-in,*
centered and loving space.

*If you are willing to **flow** with life and use only "loving communication" as your tool for implementing change, you will see **immediate** results. If you doubt this, and try to exert even a little bit of "pressure," you will again find yourself operating from an addictive space— and that just won't work without setting up new problems in your life.*

If you're going to do it and you want it to work, you have to do it right.

*Sure, if the roof leaks, you **intellectually** see the situation as being one which needs improving . . . but you **emotionally** accept it as part of the "here and now". Reacting with a negative emotion can NEVER contribute to the best possible results until you clear your head and put things in their proper perspective by letting go of the negative emotion which is caused by immediately rejecting a situation. First, every here and now situation must be accepted emotionally; then, do what your head and heart tell you to do.*

When you never get uptight about anything whatsoever, you always perform in the best possible way. It sounds like magic, doesn't it?

It may sound crazy . . . but it actually works. This is not a theory, it is an observable fact. It works every time, without exception . . . and it's a system which has proven itself over a period of thousands of years without failure.

When you give it all up [inside], you get it all back [outside].

What you give-up is your emotional attachment to a rock-like set of security, sensation and power addictions.

What you get back is a relaxed, loving, friendly world that does everything it can to love and serve you in return.

Everyone that earnestly applies this method experiences a sensation that seems like "magic." And guess what? Thousands upon thousands of people are TODAY living their lives in a state of constant happiness . . . they are emotionally accepting whatever is here and now— yes, 100% of the time. This is a fact.

And now you know how they do it.

ADDICTIVE PROGRAMING

When you uplevel all your addictions to preferences, you will discover that your body may not need as much sleep as you now require. Plus, you will have much more energy during your waking hours. You'll find that it's your addictions which make you struggle with life and cause you to needlessly expend tons of energy.

When you uplevel all your addictions to preferences, you will have insight and perceptiveness that will give you the wisdom you have always wanted—and which is now locked in your biocomputer. Up until now you haven't been able to fully use your innate wisdom simply because your powerful ego and rational mind only allowed you to see a narrow, distorted, illusory version of reality. When you tune-in to your "higher consciousness," you begin to perceive things as they are . . . not as you "think" they are.

When you are the slave of addictive programming, your ego constantly filters and rewrites your incoming sensory data and the thoughts produced by your rational mind so that you perceive only a distorted version of the world . . . one which is biased towards the security, sensation and power [control] aspects of the people and situations around you. Your biocomputer is operating in a way which constantly shortchanges you, confuses you, misleads you—and prevents your life from working properly. You see everything through the distorting filter of your programming.

When you uplevel all your addictions to preferences, you are able to LOVE EVERYONE UNCONDITIONALLY—INCLUDING YOURSELF. Your love is no longer a barter or business transaction in which you imply, "I can love you if you fit my programming. But if you don't, to hell with you. Get out of my life and stay out."

"I can love you **IF** *. . ." actually doesn't represent love at all.*

When you begin to love **everyone** *UNCONDITIONALLY—including yourself, the people around you begin to mirror your loving energy and then love you and cooperate with you in a way which they never could have done before.*

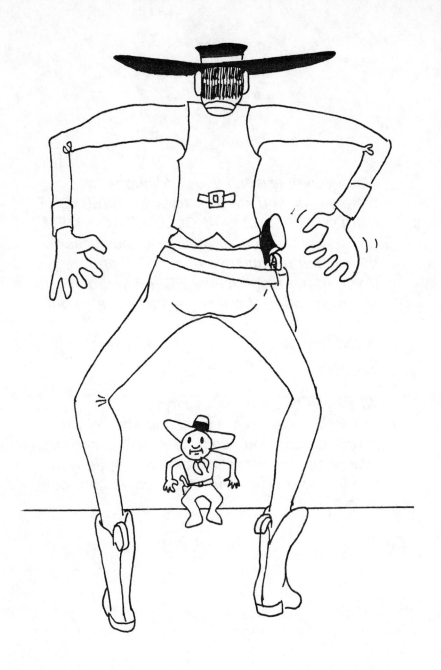

*When you try to force or manipulate people
into doing the things you want, the most you
get is surface compliance or respect—if you
are lucky. You can have respect from a person
and not have his love . . . in fact, he may
even fear you. Your life will never work if
people are afraid of you. You can never push
people into giving you love. You can't trick
them into loving you either.*

*It's love which gives energy—to you and to the
people around you—and this is the energy you really
need to make your life work well. Loving people
are happy—and happy people are loving.*

*Please realize that it's only your programming that
ever blocks you from loving someone.*

"But how can I love my enemies?" you ask.

*Well, why are they "enemies"? THEY don't perceive
themselves as "enemies". Surely their friends
don't consider them "enemies". Only your
programming makes you perceive someone as
an enemy. Change your programming and now
you can love* **everyone** *. . .*

UNCONDITIONALLY.

So now we see that by upleveling addictions to preferences, we begin to get the optimal amount of what is getable in life.

We no longer louse-up ourselves and others by trying to get what is not getable.

When we learn to love and serve everyone unconditionally, we begin to experience that life is a cornucopia which gives us far more security, sensations and power than we really need to be happy. When we don't demand or anxiously anticipate anything— **everything** *that comes along can be appreciated and enjoyed to the fullest.*

There are many great traditions for reprogramming your biocomputer and upleveling emotion-backed demands into the preferences that can enable you to flow with whatever is here and now in your life.

The method which we call the Living Love Way has been designed for us folks with big egos and well-trained rational minds.

When you use these methods, they help you get behind your ego and rational mind so that they become your faithful servants rather than your master.

Whenever you are upset and are generating the experience of unhappiness, it is because you are not following one or more of the TWELVE PATHWAYS. These PATHWAYS represent the keys to living a continuously happy, fulfilled, loving life.

Not only do these PATHWAYS define the headspace necessary for growth into "higher consciousness," they are, in themselves, an actual vehicle for growing into higher consciousness. They are the wisdom of the ages compressed into a small package for instant use whenever you are in a life situation and begin to trigger feelings of uptightness, irritation, jealousy, fear, anger, etc. Whenever you find yourself rejecting what's here and now in your life, just tune into the PATHWAY you could be using.

*We recommend that you memorize these
PATHWAYS. This will put them deep into your
biocomputer ON THE PROGRAMMING
LEVEL. If you just read them over, they will
remain a shallow, intellectual thing that will
not get at the mainspring of the basic
programming which you now use to
unconsciously trigger negative emotions.*

*Simply "understanding" them is not enough.
The Living Love Way requires that the TWELVE
PATHWAYS be PROGRAMMED deep into your
biocomputer so that they actually replace the
programming which now automatically
triggers unhappiness. When these PATHWAYS
are used as programming 100% of the
time . . . unhappiness is gone forever!*

*There is absolutely **no way** you can be
unhappy unless you are violating one or more
of the TWELVE PATHWAYS.*

*Even physical pain will not bring you
unhappiness if you use the PATHWAYS! Pain
simply represents a feeling. How you react to
that feeling is what causes unhappiness. If
you use the PATHWAYS, you can change your
reaction to the feeling.*

*So here are the TWELVE PATHWAYS that will
enable you to free yourself from all the
programming which is creating unhappiness in
your life . . .*

THE TWELVE PATHWAYS
TO UNCONDITIONAL LOVE AND HAPPINESS

Freeing Myself

1. I am freeing myself from security, sensation, and power addictions that make me try to forcefully control situations in my life, and thus destroy my serenity and keep me from loving myself and others.

2. I am discovering how my consciousness-dominating addictions create my illusory version of the changing world of people and situations around me.

3. I welcome the opportunity (even if painful) that my minute-to-minute experience offers me to become aware of the addictions I must re-program to be liberated from my robot-like emotional patterns.

Being Here Now

4. I always remember that I have everything I need to enjoy my here and now—unless I am letting my consciousness be dominated by demands and expectations based on the dead past or the imagined future.

5. I take full responsibility here and now for everything I experience, for it is my own programming that creates my actions and also influences the reactions of people around me.

6. I accept myself completely here and now and consciously experience everything I feel, think, say, and do (including my emotion-backed addictions) as a necessary part of my growth into higher consciousness.

THE TWELVE PATHWAYS
TO UNCONDITIONAL LOVE AND HAPPINESS

Interacting With Others

7. I open myself genuinely to all people by being willing to fully communicate my deepest feelings, since hiding in any degree keeps me stuck in my illusion of separateness from other people.

8. I feel with loving compassion the problems of others without getting caught up emotionally in their predicaments that are offering them messages they need for their growth.

9. I act freely when I am tuned in, centered, and loving, but if possible I avoid acting when I am emotionally upset and depriving myself of the wisdom that flows from love and expanded consciousness.

Discovering My Conscious-awareness

10. I am continually calming the restless scanning of my rational mind in order to perceive the finer energies that enable me to unitively merge with everything around me.

11. I am constantly aware of which of The Seven Centers of Consciousness I am using, and I feel my energy, perceptiveness, love and inner peace growing as I open all of the Centers of Consciousness.

12. I am perceiving everyone, including myself, as an awakening being who is here to claim his or her birthright to the higher consciousness planes of unconditional love and oneness.

That may be a pretty heavy load to pick up all at once—although you probably understood most of it quite well INTELLECTUALLY.

You will have to live with the TWELVE PATHWAYS for a while in order to appreciate their deeper significance and realize how they can affect your moment-to-moment living.*

*The TWELVE PATHWAYS are explained in greater detail in the HAND-BOOK TO HIGHER CONSCIOUSNESS. This is an easily understood, comprehensive text by Ken Keyes, Jr. This popular how-to-do-it book may be obtained in bookstores or ordered from the Living Love Center, 1730 La Loma Avenue, Berkeley, California 94709. $2.95, plus 25c for postage and handling. California residents should add 18c sales tax.

As you use this method to grow towards higher consciousness, you will become increasingly aware of the Seven Centers of Consciousness. The lowest is the Security Center, followed by the Sensation Center and then the Power Center. These lower three Centers can only produce a roller-coastering between pleasure and pain. A person who is trapped in these three Centers of Consciousness can never know continuous happiness.

When you raise your consciousness to the Fourth Center, the Love Center, you begin to experience continuous happiness in your life. The Fifth Center is known as the Cornucopia Center; here you experience the world as being a giant horn of plenty which gives you more than you will ever need to be happy at all times. Beyond that lies the exquisite Self-awareness Center and the far-out Cosmic Consciousness Center.

It is an incredibly beautiful experience to watch yourself progress from a state of occasional pleasure to a space where you can actually sense that happiness is becoming a part of your everyday life.

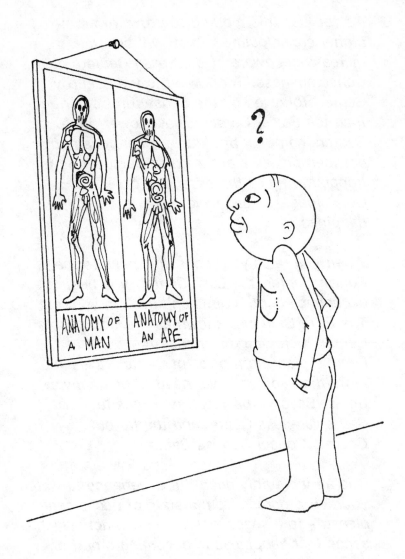

Man is a mammal; an animal.

Man, however, unlike any other animal, has a
choice of using "higher consciousness."
Lower animals are only conscious of their
[1] security; [2] sensation and [3] power needs.
Man can operate solely from these three
Centers of Consciousness as well. But Man
is the only animal who can raise his consciousness
to encompass [4] unconditional love;
[5] appreciation of life; [6] self-awareness and
[7] unity with the universe. When we speak of
using our "higher consciousness," we refer to
the four Centers which animals do not have.

Without changing his outward activities, a
man's head may be operating from Center 1, 2,
3, 4, 5, 6 or 7.

Your present life activities can be much more
fulfilling when you learn to use your higher
Centers more frequently and free yourself from
all the problems caused by your three lower
animal Centers.

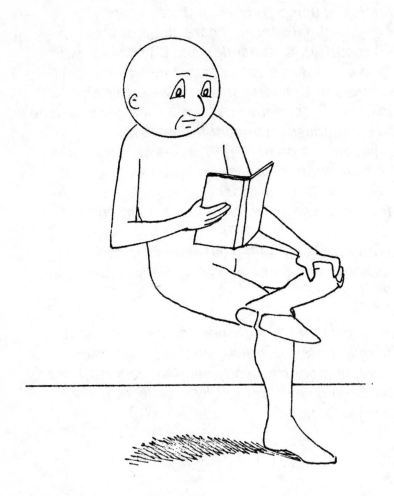

It has been said that this "secret" of happiness cannot be taught—IT HAS TO BE CAUGHT!

Are you catching it?

It's all here in this little book; but perhaps your programming, your ego and your rational mind only let you understand a tiny part of it.

That's all right, though . . . it's to be expected. So just start reading the book over again. Really! Just turn back to the beginning and start again . . . it's definitely worth it, you know. After all, we're not just talking about myths and fantasies . . . we're talking about the key to CONSTANT HAPPINESS . . . and this is a REALITY!

No kidding! This book is telling you how you can be loving and happy 100% of the time and there are lots of people DOING IT—RIGHT NOW. The next time you read this book you'll understand a little bit more.

The FIRST THING that you should tune into is seeing the connection between your suffering and your addictive programming. ALL THE NEGATIVE ASPECTS OF YOUR LIFE ARE CAUSED BY YOUR ADDICTIONS! Do you see that?

Your big breakthrough will come when you finally **experience** *that it is possible to uplevel an addiction to a preference . . . this happens when you stop blaming the outside world and see the addiction as being the TOTAL cause of your suffering.*

Part of the "magical" experience that goes
along with this method is the realization that
you CAN reprogram your biocomputer.

In fact, **you** are the only one who can do it.
Consciousness growth can only come from
deep, inner motivation and commitment—
it cannot be imposed from the outside.

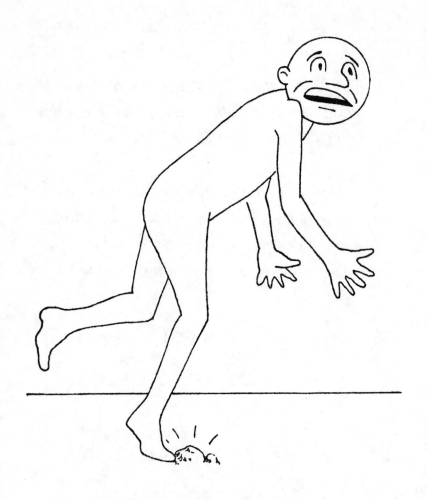

It you stumble . . . it's okay.

Just get up and go on.

DON'T BE ADDICTED TO NOT STUMBLING.

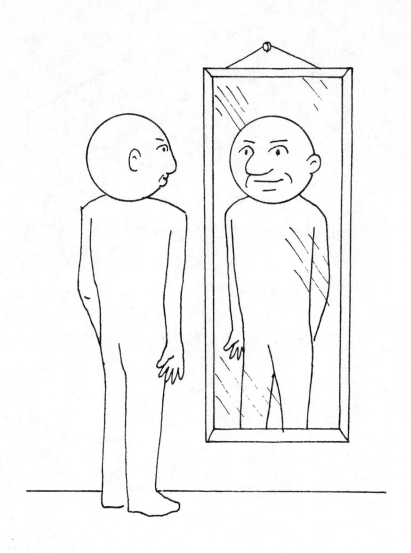

*Be patient—remember to accept yourself
COMPLETELY just as you are—here and now.
[That's the sixth PATHWAY.] If you have
addictions here and now, you have no choice
but to accept them . . . part of this method
requires that you not reject any aspect of what
is here and now.*

*Sure, you are trying to free yourself from these
addictions, but if they are part of the here and now . . .
what good will rejecting them do? Simply make a
conscious effort to experience where you are at
any given moment and get on with the work
of liberating yourself from the addictions that are
here and now. If you won't accept* **yourself** *just as
you are, you won't be able to accept the people
and situations around you . . . unconditionally!*

*It takes time—and you've got the rest of your
life to do it. Of course the faster you do it, the
quicker you will be freed from the roller-
coastering between pleasure and pain.*

So let's get on with the inner work of correcting that which makes us separate ourselves from the people and situations that are here and now in our lives.

Once you realize that it is absolutely practical and possible to create a continuously happy, loving, conscious, fulfilled life . . . nothing will stop you until you are there.

It is security, sensation and power addictions that are the germs which cause ALL social diseases: prejudice, economic exploitation, war, hatred, etc. etc. etc. You can make an enormous contribution towards solving all the world's problems [both group and individual] if you simply WORK ON YOUR OWN CONSCIOUSNESS so that you no longer spread the addictive disease germs which cause suffering throughout the world.

Don't get trapped in the phony space of trying to tell other people how they should operate their consciousness until you have successfully demonstrated it in your own life. When you yourself are free from addictions, then you will [by your own example] be able to interest other people in getting rid of their addictions. Don't use the Living Love Way as another means of manipulating and controlling the human beings around you.

Remember, too, that ethnic groups, communities and even nations have a consciousness. These large masses of people also act from security, sensation and power Centers. These group consciousnesses also have addictive programming. You can start helping them get free by working on yourself so that you can begin the inevitable upward "spiral" which will ultimately raise the consciousness of all the world's societies. Long ago it was written that "the journey of a thousand miles begins with the first step."

This book may be your first step.

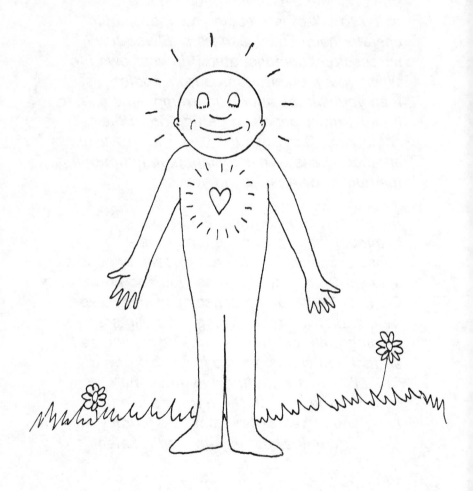

When **you** love everyone and everything in **your** life unconditionally, an inner light will illumine your hidden splendor. People may come to you, open themselves and ask you to share with them how you got rid of the disease called unhappiness.

Then, and only then, will you be able to effectively explain that the germs which cause unhappiness have been identified as belonging to the species called **"addictivus expectationus."** Then you may furnish your friends with twelve "anti-toxins" known as the TWELVE PATHWAYS which can be used to cure all unhappiness

Perhaps for the first time in your life you will deeply experience that you are playing a vital part in creating the New Age of Man.

When you use only your "higher consciousness," you are helping to eliminate the **cause** of all human suffering.

You are no longer thrashing away trying to fight the symptoms . . . expending all your energy in ways which simply cause the disease to erupt somewhere else in the social organism.

So now you know how to make your life work.

You also know how to make your society work.

What are you going to do with this knowledge?

*What will your present programming permit
you to do?*

So now you know . . .

You know how to live a loving, conscious, fulfilled life.

You know how to stop the rampant suffering that is going on throughout the world, so that coming generations can make their lives work also.

You know how to transform your inner programming so you can become the creator of a New You and a New World.

You know how to experience the wisdom, happiness and bliss that has been spoken of by all the great teachers in Time.

Life is an enjoyable game to be played—not a horrible problem to be solved.

When you uplevel your addictions to preferences, thereby reducing your ego's demands, you automatically increase your power to create a heaven which you can experience here and now on earth.

Saints and scholars have been saying this in many ways through many ages . . . No one who has found the key to happiness—the key to "heaven"—wants to keep it a secret.

"Let those who have ears to hear . . ."

LIVING LOVE

Logo by Susan Stafford

THE
LIVING LOVE CENTER

The Living Love Center is a beautiful thirty-two room home located at the foot of the Berkeley Hills in Berkeley, California. Our home, property and school are maintained by a group of people who wish to live here and study the methods of living consistently serene and happy lives by using Living Love techniques as a part of their daily life.

Since the Living Love Way is a compatible companion to any growth program, humanistic science or spiritual path which emphasizes awareness, love and oneness, many businessmen, teachers, laborers, students, doctors, housewives, clergy and professional people throughout the United States and Canada have come to Berkeley for specific instruction in using the methods described in this book.

If you are earnestly trying to improve your life and environment, please inquire about our non-profit Training Programs by writing for a brochure and calendar of coming events. You may also wish to write us for additional information on available literature, cassette recordings, specialized training sessions, lectures and out-of-state programs conducted by the Living Love Center Training Staff.

LIVING LOVE CENTER
1730 La Loma Avenue
Berkeley, California 94709

Phone: (415) 848-9341 (Closed Tuesdays)